Be A "C" Parent

STEVE STRAUGHTER

ISBN: 978-1-956618-01-3

Cover design by: Steve Straughter
Library of Congress Control Number: *Pending*
Printed in the United States of America

DEDICATION

For Mandetter & Emily
For Kelsey & Sophie
For the family I call family
For every child

CONTENTS

PREFACE

This book is the culmination of over 20 years of experience as a person that has been deeply involved with the healthy growth of children. Why did I spend so much time in this area?

That's kind of a loaded question.

I looked back over my childhood as I advanced through school and degrees and thought about how did I get here? Was it all because of my hard work? Was I genetically destined to have some sort of superior intellect? Why am I so focused on making sure children don't get their heads fucked up by adults?

I started coaching 8th graders in basketball as a 16-year-old that had just graduated from high school. Neither the parents nor the players knew how young I was, but I knew that I loved sports and I knew that I understood enough to support making this experience phenomenal for them. The goal for me at 16 was to show the players how fun the game could be.

I had no idea that this would begin a lifelong love of coaching and seeing children overcome their internal struggles and seeing parents learn how to connect with their children in new ways.

Looking back on it my childhood made a lot of difference on my path. My parent figures did some things amazingly right and amazingly wrong. I will reserve to talk about this more in another book, but for now, know I had realized that ALL parents make mistakes.

I too would have the great fortune of being a parent and

attempting to not make the same wrongs that my parents made only to find myself having to confront each decision considering what the future could indicate if I chose this or that path. Parenting is like carrying around an empty backpack on your back and along the way you have the densest rocks thrown in for every mistake or error you make along the way. By the time your child is a teenager your back and your knees are just worn out with all the mistakes that you make.

That is why I wrote this book so that new parents can have some other parts of their bodies worn out! So that your backpack can stay a bit lighter, and you will understand more than I did, or my parents did, or your parents did.

I focus on the children because all the woes of society stem from our treatment of children in my view. If I were to be methodical, and I am, I would point your attention towards some of the greatest atrocities in human existence as well as some of the greatest accomplishments. All stemmed from some origin in childhood.

Think of any feat: a championship win by a determined human that is an athlete overcoming all odds; a human that is a world leader that rises to power and commits religious genocide to an entire people; a human that is an executive that rises to power from humble beginnings only to later bankrupt an entire nation. Some humans were behind the greatest defeats and victories in war, and all found themselves acting in those positions, in some part, due to their upbringing.

Did you just stop for a minute to try to figure out who I was referring to in those statements? Good! Like art, sound writing can be left up to the interpretation of the reader and this book is reflective of such. Some of the things I mention may cause your celebration or disgust, your thoughtful approval, or judging head shakes. Regardless of how you interpret what I write this thoughtful reflection needs to happen.

Each one of us needs to take complete ownership that we alone are responsible for some action that some child will take somewhere, at some time, in the future. Yes, you are responsible. Not the video game, the neighbor, the grandparents, the teacher, the school, the political climate; the entertainment industry; the religious entity, the books, their friends, your friends: YOU. Be intentional about it. Be A "C" Parent.

Be A "C" Parent

INTRODUCTION

This book is intended and focused on the soon-to-be or new parent. It does not matter if you obtain the newborn via sexual intercourse or coitus, in vitro fertilization, or adoption this simple guide will support you in being the best parent possible for your child. If you have had a child already, and have struggled, then this small book of wisdom is for you as well.

Most of the time we become parents without having parents of our own, a poor example in our homes, or maybe we had amazing adults to model love for us. Let's just acknowledge together that there is no blueprint out there for how to get it right.

There are numerous cases where children have had it all, it appears, and nothing but the pain comes out of their testimony. There are numerous examples of adults that speak of their experience as children being a literal nightmare and they thrive in life and love because they fought for a better existence.

This book was not meant to align with heteronormativity as a foundation for all relations between humans. This book is meant to accommodate all forms of relations among partners, be it hetero-, homo-, poly-, and/or single parenting relationships.

This book attempts to remove the boundaries of genderisms allowing for all persons of any gender representation to use these nuggets of wisdom.
It's time to take off the gloves and fight for a better future for our children.

This is not political or religious-based guidance. I admit

there are plenty of books and videos in the world today that offer that sort of guidance. This is based on what has been proven to work and you will succeed as a parent by placing all of these "C's" into your toolbox.

Parts Explained

{Mental Pause for Reflection} – This will indicate that you should take whatever time is needed to think about the question or statement presented. Often, in life and school, we are not taught the science behind learning.

Many will graduate with their bachelor's degree and not once have anyone introduce to them the nuances of building a framework for learning new concepts nor extending understanding of the self. If you pause for a moment and reflect during this time, I guarantee that this simple book will have more value each time you read it.

You will find yourself sending a text or making a call or meeting for coffee to discuss what you feel and what you think; to bounce your ideas off of others.

Deep Dive – I could not, in good conscience, write any text without academic references. It is a habit of mine now to make sure to consult the literature for empirical evidence on any topic, if possible, and that is why this short area is included. Consider it to be suggested readings in the area of the topic. This is for the nerd in me and maybe the nerd in you. This is for the skeptic in me and maybe the skeptic in you.

You could skip this entire section and still find immense value in the book, and I am sure many will do just that. I mean who wants to be bored to death with cited works and reminders of days in school! Forgive me as I could not resist these little departures into the scholarly abyss.

CONCEPTUALIZE

How will we ever create limitless potential if we do not conceive of a life without limits? – Steve Straughter

How can we know where we want to go if we never set a measure of where we should be? This is the classic example that is given time and time again by those that achieve human success in their lives. Not financial success because let's be honest: there is more to life than money! Look at the recent divorces of multibillionaires Gates and Bezos; money couldn't keep them married. For you to achieve success with your newborn, or baby-to-be, you must create a concept of what parenting looks like for you!

How do I/we do that?

Let's first acknowledge what you already have in your playbook or on your blueprint or what's on your map that you might not recognize.

Real quick go ahead and give me the first example that comes to mind of people that you think are rock stars as parents.

{Mental Pause for Reflection}

As I said earlier this is not going to be about any religious or social beliefs... It may not even be about what is moral as morality changes with time.

What is timeless with conceptualization?

Having a vision of where you want your children to be in the future.

Do you want them to wake up every day with a feeling of confidence and being self-assured of their ability to win in life? If yes, then you must begin to create a vision of that in real steps.

Take steps to understand how to build that foundation for them as their parent. That means you MUST BE INTENTIONAL about making time to understand what you loved about your childhood and what you found to be challenging.

Why did you love what you loved?

{Mental Pause for Reflection}

Take that information and let's duplicate that! Why would we want to skip past what works to what hurt us and did not work? We need to dwell on what worked well! We need to know that we can identify the good stuff and making that happen again and again and again.

Is it that simple?

In some ways, yes!

Many factors go into any single feeling, but you can, with

effort, isolate when you felt the best as a child.

Was it when you felt heard? Was it when you felt protected and secure? Was it when you felt validated and knew your feelings mattered?

This is why I start with Conceptualize. How can you imagine something that you cannot fathom? We must start with the vision to lead the way for how we want our children to grow.

Take a moment to write your vision. As soon as you do this you will be ready for the next step. You cannot "unlock" the next portion of the book until you come up with that vision here.

What should I/we, include/consider in the vision for our child?

1. What do I want our children to remember from their upbringing? What values, what stories, what places, what interactions, what people?
2. What environments will help support the healthy upbringing of our child according to my values and vision?
3. Who do I want to participate in building this foundational vision for our child?
4. What am I going to do specifically to support the healthy growth of our child?
5. What things does our child need to be healthy?
6. What does it mean to be healthy?
7. Am I healthy?

{Mental Pause for Reflection}

Instead of wasting my time and yours this hard pause prevents going about reading as normal. This is an actionable approach to your success and the well-being of your child.

Writing and thinking these things out will support dialogue and may even indicate that you need to seek help to understand yourself before having a child or be in emergency mode because you have a child now and you have no clue about yourself!

To get to the next part you will have earned it!

COMMUNICATE

Some parts of our body operate without our intentionality towards it; the tongue should never fall into that category. – Steve Straughter

Did you know that this chapter does not even make sense if you have not done the really difficult work of digging into Conceptualization?

{*Hint: Go back and do the work.*}

Okay, you have arrived here after doing some intense work on reflection and creating a blueprint for how you want to see your child raised. That's awesome! Now let's roll up our mental sleeves and tackle the 2nd most important concept… the way you speak.

"I have been talking my whole life and I know how to speak to people." This is a common statement that I get when I counsel adults in this area. Here is a way for you to do a temperature check of yourself at this moment: try to remember the last time that you were frustrated, upset, angered, or downright mad and how you spoke.

{Mental Pause for Reflection}

Why was I experiencing those emotions?

This is a good first question to ask yourself because you cannot know what activates your emotions if you do not reflect on them. Why am I asking you to start there?

This simple reason: babies do not communicate like toddlers. They have no words. They just cry and scream.

If you do not have your emotions together and understand what activates you and what triggers you then the baby cannot help you figure that out.

Babies are intrinsically selfish and self-centered.

They know only what makes them feel comfortable or uncomfortable. That's it. That simple.

When the baby cries and screams they cannot fathom how that makes you feel or if you have had a long day at work or if you have self-esteem issues or if you were just broken up with or if you just got into a car accident or if you have had a death in the family.

They just don't care.

They are dealing with having gassiness, being hungry, a need to be burped, pooping and peeing, and an overload of sensory information.

What activates you and triggers you is not on their radar.

So now you're asking, "What does this have to do with Communication?"

We communicate verbally and non-verbally to everyone we meet and to ourselves. We communicate things we feel and think. In essence, your first communications with your newborn are non-verbal. This means that the way you hold them, move them, place them, and guide them tells them how they are to be treated or what is normal.

Take a second and think of the last time you saw a parent with a newborn… how long was it before you heard them say "No" or "Stop"? What do you remember hearing them say?

{Mental Pause for Reflection}

I am telling you that significant behavioral foundations are built by the communication that occurs early on in the life of your infant.

The key to communicating with your newborn is to understand yourself and actualize your limits as a person thus far and grow and mature in those areas.

The simple of it: create your own rules for what fits the concept that you designed early on.

If you do not create the rules, then you are saying that you accept society's standard for how things are done, and you are okay with not putting in the work in this area.

When you drive on a road with no lines you are operating under the assumption that all drivers will know the rules you know and stay in their lane. That could lead to a catastrophe!

What should I/we include/consider for how I or we talk to our child?

1. Is what I say to them necessary?
2. Is what I say to them true?
3. Is what I say to them kind?
4. Is this language that I am using with them reflective of their actions or my feelings?
5. Do I think the words that I am saying will cause them any harm at any point in their lives?
6. Are my non-verbal actions creating safety and security for my infant?
7. What shows should I expose my newborn to and why?
8. How will I address relatives and friends that will not respect my rules for communicating with our child?
9. Am I demonstrating through my actions how I want to teach our child to communicate?
10. How will I communicate when I fail or make mistakes with our newborn?

CONSISTENCY

If you are not willing to finish what you start, then you may not want to start anything, especially with children, because their memory is better than yours. – Steve Straughter

I think that this chapter could be an entire volume of work in parenting.

Just imagine, for a moment, if you drove a car in a major city, where the signage did not have the same meaning at all intersections. That seems absurd, right?

Think about what could go wrong.... There would, at the bare minimum, be vast amounts of confusion, chaos, and catastrophe. You know what these signs should mean because, along the way, you have had enough exposure to these signs through your senses that your brain has done the amazing work of organizing how those signs work together to form a message.

You are like a HUGE sign for your newborn!

Each action that you do, be it verbal or non-verbal, gets stored by the billions of neurons in their brain. Consider the brain to be like a road map that shows every street in the entire world and the streets are the neurons. The streets connect in most areas, but in some areas, there are dead ends.

You are the creator of every street in the brain of your newborn.

If you create a concept of how you want your baby to be then the design will consist of a roadmap that will create more healthy connections than dead ends.

Consider the common challenge that new parents have of the crying newborn. You must decide what does this crying means and then you must decide to take action.

Is their diaper soiled? Are they ill? Are they hungry? Are they congested?

That's the most difficult part about being a new parent is how to interpret what each cry means. Why can't babies come with signage?

So here you are trying to figure out with all your senses what needs to happen to stop the crying because babies do not cry with a soothing tone like your favorite singer, and you turn into the greatest detective of all time. You are sniffing, looking, listening, and talking to your baby like they understand you and are going to give you a hint.

Whatever your actions are in those moments will be like you are building a new road in your baby's mind. This is why you must be intentional in your actions towards a response to your baby. What actions were intentional in your childhood? What actions were consistent?

{Mental Pause for Reflection}

But it is not just in responses or reactions that consistency matters. It is in proactive behaviors as well.

The word routine has been given mixed reviews in society as being mundane and boring. Newborns thrive with boring! They are not here for surprises and sneak attacks on their senses.

Take a moment to appreciate how evolved you are at this point in your life. A newborn is getting trillions of sensory information at one time as everything is new to them. They feel most secure when they know something is going to happen more than once that is positive.

This is why you must be intentional about building consistency through positive routines. These routines will begin to form a structured road map that is clear and easy to read for your baby. They will begin to have expectations based on your positive and intentional routines. They will look forward to seeing you in the morning or you reading to them at night. They will find joy in your airplane sounds while feeding them or in your humming while they are drinking their milk or formula.

What should I/we include/consider in building consistency with our child?

1. What do I want our baby's overall day to look like?
2. What time will we wake our baby up?
3. What time will our baby take a nap?
4. What time will our baby go to sleep?
5. What time will our baby have playtime?
6. What will the playtime activities be?
7. What will I do to create a consistent environment

for our children?
8. How will I interact with our baby when I am frustrated about other things?
9. How will I interact with our baby when I am frustrated by our baby?
10. What processes do I need to create now that will support structure in behavior?

Ten is interesting as it will be expounded on in the next chapters. Recall in the introduction I mentioned how the greatest and most atrocious human actions are rooted in early childhood experiences. The consistency that you have with your child creates these paths. Horrific and amazing acts are not always well-publicized but within our families, we know the stories that are never told.

We know about the son that grew up to administer CPR to a baby at the beach. We know about the daughter that used sign language to lower the anxiety of a post-lingually deaf grandmother that had just been robbed. We know of a son that grew up to poison over a hundred residents in a senior living community. We know of a daughter that grew up to embezzle millions of dollars from a retirement fund they managed.

None of these have to be the outcome for any child you raise, but along the way, each adult reflects on their upbringing and decides what road they will take in the map of life based on some drawing that you assisted in creating on the map. Own it.

CHOICES

Limiting your child's options starts from conception. – Steve Straughter

Do you realize at this point that you have been given options throughout this book? Think about it....

When you looked at the cover you had to decide if you wanted to read the description. If you chose to read the description, you had to decide if you wanted to buy the book.

After you decided to read the book, you had a choice to skip the preface and introduction and jump right into the chapters. Some things happen in life that we do not realize that we had a choice in participating in or not. There are some moments when the apparent choices are obvious, and the most difficult thing is deciding which to choose.

The best parenting consists of presenting strategic choices to your child. Even as a baby you can decide to offer them a choice, in most cases, of a bottle of formula or breastfeeding or a combination of both. Had you any idea that they decide based on the choices that you offer them in this area?

It is a common practice to think of only adolescents having choices, but a wise parent starts creating a road map with directions of up or down and left or right as soon as they decide on anything. Have you ever seen a parent put a tablet or phone in front of their child? They have decided that the child will now be entertained or have their attention occupied by applications on these devices.

This is not a call to judgment on the practice of devices! These statements simply suggest that you as a parent will create choices from your decisions. If your infant becomes attached to anything it is because you decided to limit their choice of interaction with the world.

Consider the use of a thumb or a pacifier for infants that find soothing in sucking. Some new parents are adamantly opposed to their children sticking their thumbs in their mouths, so they start a pacifier early on and keep chastising their newborn if they refuse the pacifier.

The newborn knows what works though! They may have the experience of the pacifier and recall the feel of the thumb and prefer the thumb, but here you are trying to take away their preference, their choice, because of what you think is best. Think back to a time in your childhood where an adult decided for you when you felt that other options would be better.

Did you later appreciate their decision? Are you still upset that they made the choice for you and demanded your obedience?

{Mental Pause for Reflection}

Consider that you are again put in the position of the creator. You created the concept by which your newborn will operate. You created the guidelines for how you will communicate with your newborn. You created the processes for how to be consistent with your newborn. Now you are sitting again at the creator's table determining how to create choices for your newborn so that they can practice making decisions.

What you are setting them up for is a lifelong journey of critical thinking. Sure, at first it is not so critical. It is a nipple from a breast or a plastic nipple from a bottle. It is a decision on sounds and music. It is a decision on time spent with you or your partner(s) or both. Over time this becomes more important though and I posit that you are doing the best for your child by creating options early, often, and consistently.

There should be no decision that your child makes without options.

I see the eyes rolling, the laughter in mocking disdain at the thought that a newborn could even do such a thing or that you, as a responsible adult, would ever allow such a thing. I challenge you to consider the difference between the parent that leaves their infant in the cradle versus the one that allows them to roam freely.

If there is no imminent danger and all things are equal, the infant that can crawl around freely may have more opportunities to discover and make connections with the world. You make this decision for them when you are too tired or just exhausted from having to play with them or tend to them.

Recall earlier on I mentioned that newborns simply are not programmed to care about you. They care about themselves and their needs. Consider what processes you could put in place to continue to give your newborn options even when you are exhausted.

{Mental Pause for Reflection}

Are you feeling any pushback against creating options for your children?

{Mental Pause for Reflection}

Sometimes adults tend to revert to their childhood and maybe their station in life and place their newborn in a position of loss by suggesting what they have not been given. If you cannot put aside and cope with your trauma then having a child is not the opportune thing to do! Your lived trauma will have a real effect on your parenting and unless you stop and address this then you will not be able to fully create for your newborn.

Are you ready for this?

{Mental Pause for Reflection}

What should I/we include/consider in creating choices for our child?

1. Is there any harm that will come from them having a choice?

Will the choices I create for them to choose from add value to their lives?

CONSEQUENCES

What would life even be if we did not know what to expect from our actions? – Steve Straughter

Thus far we have been building a firm foundation for being a new parent that is centered on you in the equation of parenting. If you have done the work, then you have conceived of what you want for your child, laying the blueprint for their early life. You have discovered ways to communicate with them in a healthy and nurturing way. You have created a path towards consistency in how you will operate with them in every way. You have decided to create choices to build critical thinking and provide them with a head start to solve the many challenges that they will meet along the roads in their life.

Now comes the one thing that cannot stand alone: Consequences.

Maybe you start having flashbacks to your parochial days and remember learning of scientific principles such as for every action there is an equal and opposite reaction. This may also activate, depending on where you were reared, sentiments of corporal punishment in school and physical punishment at home.

Perhaps this activates for you stern anxieties of the enforcement of the law by those humans acting as officers and the traumatic scenes of murder and abuse that have lingered so effortlessly in the 365-day 24/7 news cycles through your devices. There is no doubt that the word consequence has some foundation in your memory and emotes some form of physiological response in your mind.

{Mental Pause for Reflection}

I am sorry to say that is exactly what I must ask that you consider for your newborn.

When I asked you to conceptualize what you want for your baby, I knew that in the narrow crevices of that request was a hidden note that read, "What would happen if I do not have a vision for our child?".

When I asked you to consider how you will communicate with your newborn, both verbally and non-verbally, I knew that there was another ominous undertone written in between the lines screaming at you, "What would happen if I were not intentional in how I speak with our child?".

The same goes for consistency and choices.

You see we, as adults, have been socialized to be this way. To think of consequences. When we think of consequences with intentionality, we find ourselves almost always free and clear of any nominal danger or impediment to our growth and life. That is not always the case, but for the most part that has been the promise of an unwritten social contract. If we just follow the rules, then everything will be alright.

This is why you must consider how you will explain, act on, and create consequences as a new parent. Your actions have consequences for your child. What will their actions or behaviors result in with you?

{Mental Pause for Reflection}

Let us revisit some prior work.

If you have sat in reflection on your childhood, and perhaps, even taken some time to visit with a licensed professional counselor (LPC), a psychologist (Ph.D. or Psy.D.), or a psychiatrist (M.D. or D.O.) then you are well on your way to being healthy you before doling out a poor blueprint for your child. Consider that you must first focus on yourself before you can create an objective road map for your child that is built on the best knowledge that exists. Do you want to ruin your baby's life due to you not doing the work to heal your trauma and understand your childhood?

{Mental Pause for Reflection}

So, if you are healthy and have absorbed what it means to be consistent and to create choices then consequence creation is tied directly to these two. Each choice that your baby is given will have a consequence and in the first year or so the consequence will not be solely on you as the parent as the infant will have an immediate reaction to most of their choices. They will either like the way something tastes or not. They will either find something funny or frightening. The evolution of our species has some pre-mixed reactions built into our brain structures to help us survive.

We need to pause here for a moment to address what often goes overlooked.

Consequences are not always negative! Consequences can be both positive and negative. The social construct of consequences has leaned towards more attention being given to the negative portion of the meaning but that is not the case. When considering consequences and explaining consequences to your infant it is important to share the joy in their decisions as well. Think of a time when you chose something that had positive consequences for your life.

{Mental Pause for Reflection}

Consider that if you do not present choices then you are limiting the consequences that your child will experience. You are determining for them what their outcome will be without providing them a choice. All outcomes could ultimately result in the same positive influence, but the choice instills agency in the child early on.

Also, consider that if you are not consistent in the practice of acting on consequences then you might as well scrap all of your prior work because the result for your child is going to be non-existent. What you are trying to accomplish is teaching them a lesson that whatever their actions are there will be some consequence.

As I stated earlier, this is not a religious, political, or morality-based text. These items stand on their own without any left or right side in supporting you, the new parent, in creating a lifelong roadmap for the healthy maturation of your child.

What should I/we include/consider in explaining consequences to our child?

1. Be present and recognize that when an opportunity presents itself you must speak on the matter at the

moment.

2. Am I teaching or am I yelling at our child?
3. Is my position on the matter logical or am I doing what was done to me?
4. If I were an objective party outside of the situation, how would I address the action that happened?

Am I making too much of this situation?

DEEP DIVE

There is a vast amount of scholarly literature that deals with parenting. Most of this literature is built around studies of what is measurable in terms of self-reports or observations. Let me take a step back and say that scholarly literature refers to studies that have been peer-reviewed in any academic field, such as neuroscience, early childhood development, clinical psychology, etc.

The reason why this would be of value is that, ideally, this is the way that scholars progress in their understanding of their field and how they take that information and create new theories and applications that our species can benefit from as a whole. Adding to the collective knowledge is happening at a faster rate than ever due to technology but that also means that the legitimacy of all research is not as scrutinized as it has been in the past, to some extent.

I have presented 5 broad topics in this text for you to examine as a soon-to-be or new parent. There is not a single study at the time of this publishing of this text that primarily focuses on creating a vision for your child and the outcomes that may result. This is a novel area where researchers should be focused on in parenting. Many books have been published on parenting, but the attention towards building a vision for your child's life is not the focus.

That being said there are still gems of knowledge that I recommend you add to your reading list. Simply scan the QRC code below and it will take you to my site where you will be able to read some of my latest blogs, get books I recommend, and engage in virtual calls with me through different platforms. [Password: Sekhmet_of_RA]

I hope that you will continue to engage in these topics with me and that you will add to the understanding of how being proactive in parenting makes a difference. Now there is no mistaking that a large number of our species came about because of "oops" moments, but if we want to do things better and truly be "woke" about life and the challenges that the world faces, maybe it is best to start within our own homes, with our own families.

Incorporate all of the best wisdom and advice from as many places as you can get it and while you are at it become part of the "C" parent nation!

ABOUT THE AUTHOR

Steve Straughter is just a different type of person. They do not know any limits and refuse to accept the status quo. They have worked tirelessly to make sure that each day, everything is challenged and lives with the motto to "Question Everything". Steve is working on several books for release in the next year including genres of non-fiction and fiction.

To follow Steve's work and the musings of his mind go to www.SteveStraughter.com and subscribe. There you will be able to book appearances and private readings, connect on social media, and buy merchandise.

www.ingramcontent.com/pod-product-compliance
Lightning Source LLC
Chambersburg PA
CBHW070336090426
42733CB00012B/2491